HAL•LEONARD
INSTRUMENTAL
PLAY-ALONG

Classical Solos
FOR
F Horn

15 Easy Solos for Contest and Performance

Arranged by Philip S

The enclosed audio CD is also a CD-ROM and includes:
Piano accompaniment for each solo in PDF format for printing.
Tempo Adjustment Software for use with most PC or Mac computers. Instructions included.

ISBN 978-1-61780-701-5

HAL•LEONARD®
CORPORATION
7777 W. BLUEMOUND RD. P.O. BOX 13819 MILWAUKEE, WI 53213

Visit Hal Leonard Online at
www.halleonard.com

WALTZ

F HORN

MORITZ VOGEL
Arranged by PHILIP SPARKE

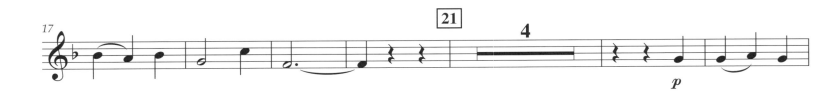

CHORALE

Now praise, my soul, the Lord

F HORN

JOHANN SEBASTIAN BACH
Arranged by PHILIP SPARKE

HUMMING SONG

from *Album for the Young*

F Horn

ROBERT SCHUMANN
Arranged by PHILIP SPARKE

GYMNOPÉDIE NO. 1

F HORN

ERIK SATIE
Arranged by PHILIP SPARKE

I'M CALLED LITTLE BUTTERCUP

from *HMS Pinafore*

F HORN

SIR ARTHUR SULLIVAN
Arranged by PHILIP SPARKE

6

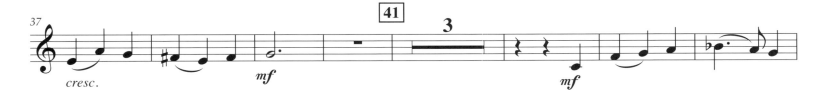

00842549

STUDY

Op. 37, No. 3

F HORN

HENRY LEMOINE
Arranged by PHILIP SPARKE

Moderato (♩ = 100)

MINUET

(Z. 649)

F HORN

HENRY PURCELL
Arranged by PHILIP SPARKE

rit.

THEME AND VARIATION

from *Sonatina No. 3*

F HORN

THOMAS ATTWOOD
Arranged by PHILIP SPARKE

Moderato (♩ = 104)

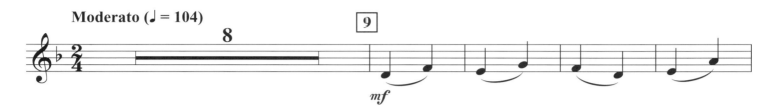

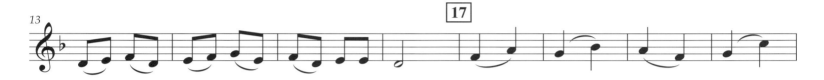

NORTHERN SONG

from *Album for the Young*

ROBERT SCHUMANN
Arranged by PHILIP SPARKE

F HORN

Moderato (♩ = 94)

TWO GERMAN DANCES

from *Twelve German Dances, D. 420*

F HORN

FRANZ SCHUBERT
Arranged by PHILIP SPARKE

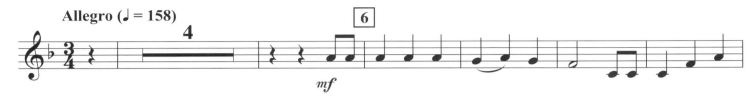

WATCH MAN'S SONG

from *Lyric Pieces, Op. 12*

F HORN

EDVARD GRIEG
Arranged by PHILIP SPARKE

Moderato (♩ = 104)

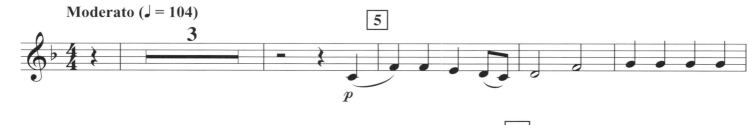

rit.

GAVOTTE

F HORN

JAN LADISLAV DUSSEK
Arranged by PHILIP SPARKE

00842549

VIEN QUÀ, DORINA BELLA

F HORN

ANTONIO BIANCHI
Transcribed by **C. M. von WEBER**
Arranged by PHILIP SPARKE

MINUET

from *Notebook for Anna Magdalena Bach*

F HORN

Attributed to **CHRISTIAN PETZOLD**
Arranged by PHILIP SPARKE

THE PRINCE OF DENMARK'S MARCH

from *Choice Lessons for the Harpsichord or Spinet*

F HORN

JEREMIAH CLARKE
Arranged by PHILIP SPARKE

(2nd time only)

rit.